KILLER CREATURES

TIGER

ANNA CLAYBOURNE

Belitha Press

▲ A male Bengal tiger opens his mouth to roar, showing his long teeth.

Produced by Monkey Puzzle Media Ltd, Gissing's Farm, Fressingfield, Suffolk IP21 5SH, UK

First published in the UK in 2001 by
Belitha Press
An imprint of Chrysalis Books plc
64 Brewery Road, London N7 9NT

Paperback edition first published in 2002

ISBN 1 84138 304 X (hardback)
ISBN 1 84138 383 X (paperback)

British Library Cataloguing in Publication Data for this book is available from the British Library.

Printed in Hong Kong

10 9 8 7 6 5 4 3 2 1

Acknowledgements
We wish to thank the following individuals and organizations for their help and assistance and for supplying material in their collections: Anna Claybourne 30; Bruce Coleman Collection 3 (John Shaw), 12 top (Gunter Ziesler), 12 bottom (J Zwaenepoel), 14–15 (J Zwaenepoel), 20 top (Leonard Lee Rue), 20 bottom (Staffan Widstrand), 26 (Staffan Widstrand); Natural Visions 10 bottom (Heather Angel), 16 top (Heather Angel); NHPA back cover top (Andy Rouse), back cover right (Andy Rouse), 1 (Martin Wendler), 4 bottom (Laurie Campbell), 6 bottom (Andy Rouse), 8 top (Roger Tidman), 8 bottom (James Warwick), 9 (Martin Harvey), 14 (Andy Rouse), 16 bottom (Andy Rouse), 17 top (Martin Harvey), 28 (James Warwick), 29 (James Warwick), 32 (Martin Harvey); Oxford Scientific Films front cover (Mahipal Singh), 6 top (Mike Brown), 10 top (Vivek Sinha), 13 (Belinda Wright), 15 (Ken Cole/Animals Animals), 17 bottom (Dani-Jeske/Animals Animals), 18 (Belinda Wright), 18–19 (Alan & Sandy Carey), 21 (Vivek Sinha), 22 bottom (Frank Schneidermeyer), 23 (Mahipal Singh), 24 top (Belinda Wright), 25 (Konrad Wothe); Stone back cover left (Schafer & Hill), 2 (Tim Flach), 4 top (James Balog), 5 (James Balog), 11 (John Garrett), 22 top (Schafer & Hill), 24 bottom (Renee Lynn).

All artwork by Michael Posen.

CONTENTS

LOOK FOR THE TIGER BOX

Look for the little black tiger in boxes like this.
Here you will find extra tiger facts, stories and
other interesting information!

THE BIGGEST CAT

Tigers are the biggest, most powerful cats in the world. Like lions, leopards and other big cats, they are good hunters, with strong muscles, long claws and sharp teeth. But tigers are very rare, and may soon disappear completely!

There are five types of tigers: Siberian (or Amur), Bengal, Indochinese, South China and Sumatran. They all belong to the same species (*Panthera tigris*), and look similar. The main difference between them is their size.

▲ A fully grown tiger can move from a standstill to more than 50 km/h in just three seconds!

🐆 IS YOUR PET LIKE A TIGER?

Although they're so big, tigers belong to the same animal family as domestic cats. They lick themselves clean, yawn, curl up in a ball to sleep, and swish their tails when they are angry – just like a pet cat or kitten.

◀ Some Bengal tigers are born with white fur, chocolate-brown stripes and blue eyes. You might see a white tiger like this one in a zoo.

Siberian or Amur tigers are the biggest, growing up to 3.3m long. Sumatran tigers are the smallest. They are usually between 2 and 2.5m long. Male tigers are always bigger than females of the same type.

Until about 70 years ago, there were three other types of tigers: Bali tigers, Javan tigers, and Caspian tigers. They have now died out.

WHERE TIGERS LIVE

In the wild, tigers live in Russia, China, India and other parts of Asia. The big map shows which tigers live where. There are also thousands of tigers living in zoos all over the world.

Wild tigers like to live in forests, where they can hide among the trees and tall grasses, and hunt other forest animals such as deer and wild boar.

They also live near rivers or lakes, so that they can lie in the water to cool down in hot weather.

Tigers usually live alone, and each tiger needs a space, or territory, to roam around and go hunting in. That's why tigers are usually found in wild places, far from cities and towns.

▲ This tiger is peering out from between some leafy branches. Tigers need lots of cover, such as long grass, forest trees and thick undergrowth, to hide in.

◄ This Bengal tiger has found the perfect place to cool off. As he charges through this shallow water, his coat gets a nice cool drenching.

BUT CATS HATE WATER!

Not tigers! They love to bathe and play in cool water, and some tigers even go paddling in the sea. Tigers are also good swimmers, which means it's easy for them to cross rivers.

This map of the world shows the tiger's natural range, which means the parts of the world where tigers live in the wild. The tiger's range used to be much bigger, stretching across all of China and India, and reaching as far as Turkey. It has shrunk because people have cut down forests and used the land to build towns, cities and farms.

Siberian tigers live in eastern Russia.

South China tigers live in China.

Indochinese tigers live in China, Thailand, Myanmar, Cambodia, Laos, Vietnam and Malaysia.

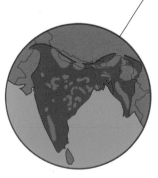

Bengal tigers live in India.

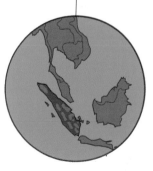

Sumatran tigers live on the island of Sumatra in Indonesia.

◀▲ The orange shading on these maps shows areas where tigers live today.

A TIGER'S DAY

Tigers are nocturnal. This means they rest during the day and are active at night.

▲ This tiger is enjoying a snooze in a pile of dry leaves and bark.

▼ After waking up from her daily sleeping session, a tiger takes a stroll around her territory.

Just like pet cats, tigers spend most of their day chilling out. They lie and doze in the long grass or in a shady cave. Or, if it's a very hot day, they wallow around in water.

Why do tigers spend so much time resting? The answer is that resting saves energy, and cuts down on the amount of food the tiger has to catch.

At dusk, it's time for tigers to get up. A typical tiger spends most of the night wandering around its territory and guarding it from other tigers.

 **FRIEND OR FOE?**

Male tigers often fight off other male tigers so that they can keep their territory to themselves. But female tigers are a bit more friendly. They sometimes share food or bathe in a pond together.

A tiger guards its territory by scratching marks on trees and bushes, and scenting them with urine, droppings or special chemicals from glands on its face and toes. These signs warn other tigers to stay away.

If the tiger is lucky, it will also manage to kill a deer, buffalo or other animal to eat. Or it might go back to an animal it's already killed and eat some more. Tigers usually keep eating until they're really full. Then, when morning comes, it's time for another rest!

▲ This tiger has bumped into a stranger while having a swim.

TIGER SENSES

Because tigers roam at night, they need extra-sharp senses to help them find their way around and catch their prey.

▲ Excellent vision and hearing help a tiger find its way at night.

During the day, a tiger's eyesight is about as good as a human's. But at night, tigers can see six times better than people can.

In the dark, a tiger's pupils can open very wide to let in lots of light. Like many other predators, tigers also have a special layer at the back of each eye, called the tapetum, which helps them see in the dark.

Light comes in through the pupil and goes through the retina at the back of the eye.

The tapetum is like a layer of shiny tinfoil behind the retina. It reflects the light patterns back though the retina.

► This diagram shows a tiger's eye cut in half, so you can see how a tiger's night vision works.

The retina collects light patterns and sends them to the tiger's brain.

EXTRA NOSE

One reason tigers are so good at smelling is that they have two noses! The second 'nose' is called Jacobson's organ. It's a sensitive patch inside the tiger's mouth, just under its real nose. A tiger uses its Jacobson's organ to work out what other tigers' scent markings mean.

As well as amazing night vision, tigers have very good hearing. They can swivel their ears around to listen for deer or other animals rustling through the forest.

Tigers don't usually use their noses to find their prey. Instead, they use scent to send each other messages – such as 'keep away from my territory!' or 'I'm looking for a mate'. A tiger can tell, just from another tiger's smell, whether it's a friend or an enemy, or a male or a female.

When a tiger is upset, it twists its ears around to show these white spots.

Light reflected from the back of the eye can make a tiger's eyes seem to glow in the dark.

Sensitive ears can twist around to listen out for prey.

Big nostrils help the tiger sniff out smelly messages from other tigers.

Long whiskers help the tiger feel its way through cave entrances and between bushes.

A tiger sometimes opens its mouth wide to sniff at a scent marking with its Jacobson's organ.

TIGER STRIPES

Have you ever wondered why tigers have stripes? It's not just so we can tell lions and tigers apart! Scientists think a tiger's stripes give it camouflage and help it to hide in the forest.

Lots of animals have camouflage, which means they can hide by blending in with their background. Where tigers live, there are lots of trees and tall grasses. The tiger's up-and-down stripes blend in with the forest and make the tiger very hard to see – especially if it's standing still.

But if tigers are so big and fierce, why do they need to hide? So that they can creep up on their prey without being seen! Then, when they are close enough, they can move in for the kill.

▲ The tiger's stripes match its natural habitat of long grass, trees and forest undergrowth.

◄ Can you spot the tiger in this picture?

 TIGER PATTERNS

Tiger stripes are like human fingerprints – no two tigers have exactly the same pattern. Some tigers even have stripes on their foreheads that look like the Chinese wang symbol, which means 'king' in Chinese writing. So it's really the tiger, not the lion, who is king of the jungle!

You might think tigers are quite easy to spot, because they're bright orange. But although tigers can see in colour, many prey animals, like deer and wild cattle, see in black and white. So to them, a stalking tiger looks even more like the trees.

▼ This tiger has a 'wang' mark. The pattern on its forehead looks a bit like the Chinese wang symbol, which stands for 'king'.

DEADLY HUNTER

A tiger catches its prey by stalking it. This means it creeps closer and closer, slowly and quietly, until it's close enough to pounce.

Tigers can run fast over a short distance, but they can't run for a long time, like a cheetah can. So they need to be as close as they can to their prey before they start running. The skill of stalking is to move so slowly and silently that the prey doesn't spot the tiger until it's too late.

▲ When a tiger has crept to about 10m away from its prey, it suddenly rushes forward.

▶ The tiger leaps on the prey, dragging it to the ground with its sharp claws and killing it by biting it on the neck or throat.

The tiger has some terrifying tools for killing its prey. It has 18 big, sharp claws – five on each front foot and four on each back foot. Each claw is up to 10 cm long. Tigers can retract their claws and hide them away in their paws, just like a pet cat.

WIN SOME, LOSE SOME

The pictures on this page show a tiger making a successful kill. But the prey often hears the tiger coming and runs away. In fact, most tigers only manage to catch one animal for every 20 times they pounce.

A fully grown tiger also has 30 big teeth. The longest are the canines, which are used for slicing through meat. They can grow up to 9 cm long.

▼ This roaring tiger is showing almost all of its teeth, including four huge canines.

TIGER FOOD

Tigers will eat just about anything, as long as it's meat. In fact, tigers are the biggest land animals that survive on nothing but meat. To do this, they have to eat a lot.

After killing its prey, a tiger drags the body to a quiet spot and eats as much as it can. Big tigers sometimes gobble up to 30 kg of meat in one go. Tigers don't chew, they just tear off chunks of meat and swallow them whole.

If the prey is too big to eat in one night, the tiger will return every night for more, until it's all gone. Then the tiger rests for a couple of days before going hunting again.

▲ This tiger is tearing a strip of meat from a deer that it has just killed.

▶ A tiger takes a drink at a fresh-water pool. Like all cats, the tiger uses its rough tongue to lap up liquids.

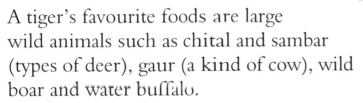

► These deer, called chital, are one of the things tigers most like to eat.

A tiger's favourite foods are large wild animals such as chital and sambar (types of deer), gaur (a kind of cow), wild boar and water buffalo.

   If they can't find large animals, tigers will also snack on monkeys, frogs and anything else that looks tasty. Because tigers spend a lot of time in water, they sometimes snap up a few fish as well.

   Tigers that live in zoos are fed about 4 kg of raw meat every day, with extra vitamins added to it.

DO TIGERS EAT PEOPLE?

Tigers rarely eat people, but it can happen. If a tiger is injured or very old, it could be too weak to catch wild animals. So it may wander into a village to look for other prey – which could mean a person, or a farm animal like a sheep. There is also a swampy area called the Sunderbans, in Bangladesh and India, where tigers have attacked several people – but no one knows why.

◄ These fishermen in the Sunderbans are wearing masks on the backs of their heads to scare tigers away.

A TIGER'S LAIR

You might have heard of a tiger's lair or a tiger's den. But in fact, tigers don't need a den to hide in, apart from when they are tiny cubs. A tiger's home is really the whole area, or territory, it lives in.

A tiger's home territory is much bigger than a den or a zoo enclosure. A female Bengal tiger has a territory of about 30 km². Male tigers' territories are even bigger – up to 120 km².

The size of a territory depends on how much food there is. If there are lots of prey animals around, tiger territories are smaller. But in cold, snowy parts of Russia, where Siberian tigers live, tiger territories have to be huge – as big as 325 km².

▼ This tiger is peering out from her den, which is a cave on a rocky ledge.

◀ These two tigers are fighting over a patch of territory. One of them will probably give in and run away without getting badly hurt.

🐆 A TIGER'S DEN

Tigers sometimes make a den in a cave, a sheltered spot between some rocks, or a clump of long grass. A den can be a good place to have a sleep, or sit and watch the world go by. But its most important use is as a shelter for newborn cubs. You can find out more about tiger cubs on page 22.

Tigers like to live alone, so they warn other tigers to keep away from their territories by scratching trees and leaving scent markings wherever they go.

Male tigers only try to scare away other male tigers, and females only keep other females off their patch. A male and a female tiger can share the same land. That way, they can sometimes meet up to mate and have cubs.

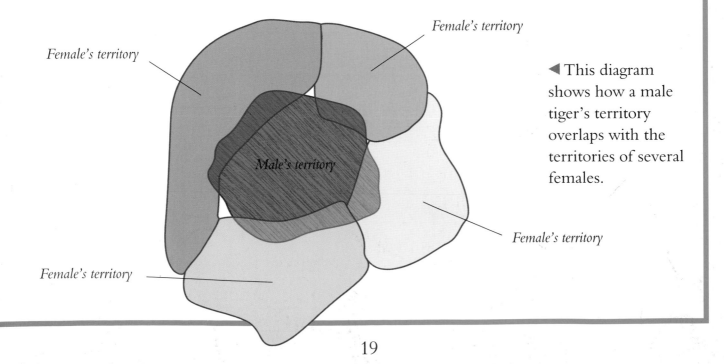

Female's territory

Female's territory

Male's territory

Female's territory

Female's territory

◀ This diagram shows how a male tiger's territory overlaps with the territories of several females.

FINDING A MATE

▲ A male tiger sniffs the air for the scent of a female.

▼ A female tiger roars to help the nearest male to find her.

Male and female tigers don't live together. So when they want to mate and have babies, they have to find each other first.

When a female tiger is ready to have cubs, she needs to tell a male tiger to come and find her. But because tiger territories are so big, the nearest male could be a long way away. To solve this problem, tigers use their favourite way of sending messages – with scent.

TIGER SOUNDS

As well as smells, tigers talk to each other by making noises. A tiger's loudest roar can be heard more than 3 km away, so it's a good way for tigers to find each other quickly. When they meet up to mate, male and female tigers also make a friendly grunting noise, which is called 'prusten'.

▼ A male and female tiger play together before mating. They rub their faces together and roll around.

The female leaves a special kind of scent on the trees and bushes around her territory. When a male finds it, he starts looking out for her. The female also roars very loudly to let him know where she is.

At last the two tigers find each other. But they don't stay together for long – only about five days. During that time, they play together and mate several times.

Then the male goes away and leaves the female to look after the cubs on her own. They are born after a gestation period, or pregnancy, of about 100 days.

TIGER CUBS

Tigers usually have two or three cubs at a time, but there could be just one cub, or as many as six. They are born in a den – a sheltered spot in a cave or a clump of long grass.

▲ The three cubs in this picture are about one month old. They are still young enough to have blue eyes.

Newborn tiger cubs weigh about a kilogram and are no bigger than a pet cat. They are weak, helpless and blind. Their eyes, are bright blue and open after a few days, but they can't see properly until they are two months old.

Tigers, like humans, are mammals, which means they feed their newborn babies with milk. The cubs start to eat meat when they are about two months old. Their mother leaves them alone in their den while she goes out hunting to find food.

▼ This tiger cub is practising stalking – probably by sneaking up on one of his brothers or sisters.

The cubs are in danger when they are not with their mother. Snakes, leopards and wild dogs will eat them if they find the cubs alone. The mother has to hurry back as fast as she can when she has caught some prey.

◀ This two-year-old cub is now bigger than his mother. It will soon be time for him to find his own place to live.

At about six months old, the cubs start to go on hunting trips with their mother. They learn to stalk and pounce by watching her. Then they practise by stalking small birds or insects, or pouncing on their mother's tail!

Female tigers have a new litter of cubs every two years. So, when they are two years old and fully grown, cubs have to make space for their little brothers and sisters. They gradually move away and find their own territories.

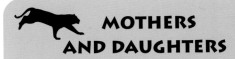 **MOTHERS AND DAUGHTERS**

Scientists have found that male cubs travel a long way from home to find a new territory, while female cubs stay close to their mothers. Often, mother and daughter tigers have territories next door to each other.

TIGERS IN DANGER

Even though tigers are so big and powerful, they are in great danger. Experts think there are now fewer than 6000 tigers left in the wild, and they could soon become extinct.

◀ A ranger plays with an orphaned baby tiger at a tiger reserve in India.

▼ The tiger is known for its strength and bravery. Some people think that if they eat medicines made of tigers, they will be strong and brave too.

Here are the main reasons why the tiger is at risk of dying out:

Habitat loss The places that the tiger likes to live in are disappearing all across Asia, because people have cut down forests to make space for farms and roads.

WILL TIGERS DIE OUT?

If tiger numbers keep shrinking, wild tigers could die out in less than 10 years. But people are making efforts to save them. There are now several tiger reserves, where tigers can live in safety, protected from poachers. Tigers are also being bred in zoos, so that even if they do die out in the wild, there will still be some left. You can find out more about saving tigers on page 30.

Safety When their habitats shrink, tigers don't have enough space or enough food. So they're more likely to attack farm animals or even people. Scared villagers shoot tigers.

Poaching This is a big problem for tigers. For a long time, rich people hunted tigers for fun. Hunting tigers is now banned, but poaching (illegal hunting) still happens, because a dead tiger is worth a lot of money. Its body parts can be sold to make Chinese medicines.

Scientists think these 'medicines' don't work very well. But lots of people still want to use them. This is partly because of a myth that says you can gain some of the tiger's strength and courage by eating its body parts.

▲ This street trader in China is selling medicines made out of tiger parts.

TIGER FACTS

Here's a selction of useful tiger facts and figures, interesting information, and tiger stories, myths and legends.

▲ The Hindu goddess Durga riding a tiger.

Biggest ever tiger
The biggest tiger recorded was a male Siberian tiger. He weighed 466 kg and was almost 4m long.

Age
In the wild, tigers usually live to between 10 and 15 years old. Tigers kept in zoos can sometimes grow as old as 25.

Teeth
An adult tiger has 30 teeth.

Claws
Tigers have 18 claws, five on each front foot and four on each back foot.

Fur
A tiger's fur is shortest on its back and longest on its stomach. Tigers who live in cold places, such as Siberia, have the longest fur – from 4 cm long on the back to 10 cm long on the stomach.

Running and jumping
The tiger's top running speed is about 55 km/h. They can also jump distances of up to 9m.

How many cubs?
Tigers have between one and six cubs in each litter. A female could have four or five litters in her lifetime. Only half of all tiger cubs born in the wild survive to be adults.

Tail length
The tiger's tail takes up about a third of its body length. So if a tiger is 3m long, its tail is about 1m long.

Tiger sizes

This chart gives the average sizes of tigers, from the tip of the nose to the tip of the tail.

Tiger type	Average size	
	Male	Female
Siberian	3m	2.6m
Bengal	2.9m	2.5m
Indochinese	2.7m	2.4m
South China	2.5m	2.3m
Sumatran	2.4m	2.2m

▲ How a large male tiger compares in size to a family car.

Collective noun

A collective noun is a name for a group. A group of tigers is known as 'a streak of tigers'.

Extinct tigers

There are three extinct types of tiger: the Javan tiger, the Bali tiger and the Caspian tiger.

The Javan tiger could grow up to 2.5m long and lived on the Indonesian island of Java. It last was spotted in 1972.

The Bali tiger lived on Bali, another Indonesian island. It was quite small, and only grew up to about 2.3m long. It disappeared in 1937.

The Caspian tiger lived in the area around the Caspian Sea, in Turkey, Iran, Afghanistan, Mongolia and parts of Russia. It was a large tiger, growing up to 3m long. Experts think it died out in the 1950s.

Tiger beliefs

In the lands where it lives, the tiger has an important role in local beliefs and folktales. In China, it stands for strength, bravery and fear. Parents used to tell their children that if they misbehaved, the Tiger Woman would eat them.

In India, the Hindu goddess Durga is said to ride a tiger. You can see her in the picture on the opposite page.

The Warli people of western India worship a tiger god called Vaghadeva.

Year of the tiger

In the Chinese calendar, every twelfth year is a year of the tiger. At a tiger New Year, children wear tiger stripes on their foreheads. People born in the year of the tiger are said to be bold and daring.

SABRE-TOOTHED TIGER

The sabre-toothed tiger, or *Smilodon*, was a prehistoric big cat which died out about 11 000 years ago. It was about 1.5m long, with two huge canine teeth up to 18 cm long. Although it was quite small, it was a fierce killer. But despite its name, *Smilodon* was not a close relative of today's tigers, and they did not evolve from it.

▶ This is how *Smilodon* may have looked.

TIGER WORDS

A young tiger shows its canine teeth.

This glossary explains some of the more unusual words you might have seen in this book.

camouflage
Patterns, colours or shapes that help an animal blend in with its background, making it harder to see.

canine teeth
Sharp, pointed teeth used for tearing meat. Many animals have them, including tigers and humans. Your canines are the two pointed teeth on either side of your four front teeth.

cheetah
A big cat found in parts of Asia and Africa. Cheetahs are not as big as tigers, but can run much faster – up to 113 km/h.

domestic
To do with human homes. A domestic cat is a cat that lives with humans in their houses.

enclosure
A large cage or fenced area. Most animals in zoos live in enclosures.

endangered
In danger of becoming extinct (see below). The tiger is just one of many endangered animal species, or types.

evolve
To change gradually over many generations. Scientists think that animal species evolve over time to suit their habitats.

extinct
Gone for ever. An extinct animal is one that has died out and will never exist again.

fossil
A rock cast of the bones or other remains of an animal or plant that died a very long time ago. Over time, as the bones rot away, they are replaced by minerals and end up as rock.

gaur
A type of wild cow which tigers like to eat.

gestation period
The amount of time a female animal spends being pregnant, before giving birth to her babies.

gland
A small organ in an animal's body that makes chemicals. For example, glands on a tiger's face and paws make scent for marking trees with. Glands in the skin on your feet make smelly sweat!

habitat
The place an animal likes to live in. The tiger's favourite habitat is a forest or swamp.

Jacobson's organ
A sensitive patch on the roof of a tiger's mouth, used for sniffing other tiger's scent markings.

litter
A set of cubs, or other baby animals, all born at the same time.

mammal
A type of animal that feeds its babies on milk. Tigers and humans are both mammals.

range
The parts of the world where an animal species is found. The tiger's range stretches across parts of India, China, Russia and Southeast Asia.

reserve
An area of land set aside for wildlife to live in safely.

poaching
Illegal hunting. Poachers kill tigers and sell their skins and body parts, even though doing so is against the law.

predator
An animal that hunts and kills other animals for food.

prey
An animal that is hunted by a predator.

prusten
An unusual noise, somewhere between grunting and clicking, which tigers make to show they're being friendly.

pug mark
A name for a tiger's paw print.

sambar
A large deer found in Asia and often eaten by tigers.

▲ A sambar, one of the tiger's favourite foods

species
A type of plant or animal. All tigers belong to one species, which has the Latin name *panthera tigris*.

sponsor
To pay for something, usually for a good cause. When you sponsor a tiger, you pay some money towards caring for it.

stalk
To follow or approach something quietly and carefully. Tigers stalk their prey, to get as close as possible before attacking.

symbol
Something that stands for something else. In Chinese writing, symbols are pictures that stand for words.

tapetum
A silvery layer at the back of a tiger's eye. It reflects light and helps the tiger see in the dark.

territory
The area of land a tiger lives in and defends as its home.

wild boar
A type of wild pig found in forests.

TIGER PROJECTS

If you want to know even more about tigers, here are some more ideas and things to do.

SEE A REAL TIGER

It's very hard to see a wild tiger, even if you go to the right parts of Asia, because they are so rare. But there is a huge international scheme to breed tigers in zoos. In fact, there are now more tigers in zoos than there are in the wild.

To find out where your nearest tiger is, look for zoos or safari parks in your telephone directory. You can also find these through tiger sites on the World Wide Web (see opposite page). Then call the zoo to find out if they have a tiger, and the best time to see it. (Remember to ask the person who is paying for the phone call first!)

▼ This photo was taken at the tiger enclosure at Edinburgh Zoo in Scotland.

TAKE A TIGER PHOTO

Tigers spend a lot of time asleep, but if you're lucky they might be eating, playing or strolling around when you visit the zoo. To take a good tiger photo, get as close as you can to the tiger (without climbing over the fence!). The tigers will still be some distance away, so use a zoom function if your camera has one.

HELP SAVE THE TIGER

It can be sad to see tigers stuck in cages or safari parks, but experts hope that by breeding tigers in captivity, they will be able to stop tigers from becoming extinct. The money you pay to visit the zoo or park helps to save tigers in this way.

Many zoos also have adoption or sponsorship schemes, which let you pay some money towards the care of a particular species. The zoo sends you a photo of your animal and updates on how he or she is getting on. They sometimes put your name on a list of sponsors next to the animal's enclosure.

It's expensive to sponsor a tiger, so why not ask if your school or your class could raise the money to help save a tiger?

TIGERS ON THE WEB

If you have access to the Internet, there are lots more fun ways to find out about and help tigers. Here are a few websites to try:

ALL ABOUT TIGERS
Tiger Information Center
http://www.5tigers.org/
Seaworld Tiger Page
http://www.seaworld.org/tiger/tigers.html
Tiger Fact Sheet
http://www.dscf.demon.co.uk/fact3.htm

TIGER FUN
National Geographic Cyber Tiger – look after a tiger and build him an enclosure.
http://www.nationalgeographic.com/tigers/maina.html
Tiger Territory – read lots of amazing fun facts and hear tiger sounds.
http://www.oberlin.k12.oh.us/prospect/jmemmott/Tiger%20Territory/!tmain.htm

Minnesota Zoo's Tigercam – see live pictures of a tiger enclosure.
http://www.mnzoo.com/partners/mnzoo/tigercam.html

HELP SAVE TIGERS
World Wildlife Fund's Endangered Species Tiger Page
http://www.worldwildlife.org/species/species.cfm?sectionid=120&newspaperid=21

Remember that the Web can change, so don't worry if you can't find all these websites when you look for them. You can do a search for other tiger sites using any search engine. Include the words 'panthera tigris' (the tiger's Latin name) in your search to make sure you don't get too many other sites about sports teams, products and companies that also use the name 'tiger'.

INDEX